NATIONAL
GEOGRAPHIC

Jupiter
The Moon King

PATHFINDER EDITION

By Beth Geiger and Ray Villard

CONTENTS

Jupiter
The Moon King

Jupiter, the fifth planet from our sun, holds many out-of-this-world records. For one thing, Jupiter is huge. It's the largest planet in our solar system. Nearly 1,400 Earths could fit inside it.

Jupiter also boasts more moons than any other planet. It is made out of gases. And it has a ring, fierce tornadoes, and raging hurricanes. All this makes Jupiter quite different from our cozy little Earth.

Jupiter looms above Ganymede.

Galileo

Giant Jupiter

Despite its tremendous size, Jupiter moves fast. It **rotates,** or spins, every ten hours. So days on Jupiter are short.

Days may be short, but Jupiter has long years. The planet is farther from our sun than Earth, so it takes longer to **revolve,** or go around the sun. It takes about 12 Earth years for Jupiter to complete its orbit.

Many Moons

Perhaps Jupiter's most amazing quality is its collection of moons. At least 63 moons orbit the giant world. There may be more. After all, 21 were found in 2002 and 2003.

Most of the moons are small. Many are just a few miles across. By far, the largest—and weirdest—are four moons discovered nearly 400 years ago. They were first spotted by an Italian scientist named Galileo (gah lih LAY oh). So they're often called the Galilean moons. Let's take a closer look at them.

Io

Io is closer to Jupiter than the other Galilean moons. Jupiter's **gravity** pulls Io toward the giant planet. Gravity from the other Galilean moons tugs Io in the opposite direction.

All the pulling and tugging creates a lot of heat on Io. The heat has caused volcanoes to erupt. Io has more volcanoes than any other planet or moon in our solar system.

Dozens of volcanoes might erupt at any time. The eruptions can be seen from space. Some of the material blasted from the volcanoes flies 190 miles above the moon's molten surface.

Europa

Europa is the next Galilean moon out from Jupiter. Unlike Io, Europa is a really cool place. In fact, a ten-mile-thick layer of ice blankets it.

The icy surface is very smooth. Heat caused by gravity melts the ice, which then flows over other features.

Beneath Europa's smooth, icy shell is a huge ocean. It may be nearly 50 miles deep. This hidden ocean could hold an amazing secret.

Some scientists think that **bacteria,** or germs, may swim in Europa's icy waters. That means life could dwell in the moon's ocean.

Ganymede

Nearly 3,300 miles across, Ganymede is huge. In fact, it's the largest moon in our solar system. It is larger than Earth's moon. And it's even bigger than a planet—Mercury.

Like Europa, Ganymede has a deep ocean. But scientists think the water is too cold for life. A thick layer of ice covers the ocean. For billions of years, **meteorites** have slammed into the ice, forming craters.

Callisto

Rock and ice are Callisto's main ingredients. Callisto is Jupiter's second largest moon.

Freckles seem to cover the moon's surface. They're actually hundreds of meteorite craters. In fact, Callisto has more craters than anything else yet found in space.

Shining Light on Moons

For years, the planets in our solar system got all the attention. Now some scientists are focusing on moons. It's about time.

Moons, after all, can be as weird and wonderful as the planets they orbit. On just four, you've seen volcanoes, oceans, ice, and craters. Who knows what we'll see next?

If you could explore one of Jupiter's moons, which one would you pick? Why?

Flyby. *The Galileo spacecraft flies toward Jupiter.*

Wordwise

bacteria: germs
gravity: force that pulls objects together
meteorite: rock from space that has crashed on a planet or moon
revolve: to go around
rotate: to spin on an axis

Moonlight. *Ganymede is larger and has more craters than Earth's moon.*

Pizza Moon. *Io has so many active volcanoes that the moon is turning itself inside out. All this makes the moon look like a pizza.*

Fire and Ice. *Meteorites have blasted thousands of craters into Callisto's icy surface.*

Our Solar System

Out-of-This-World Facts

- Mercury and Venus are the only planets in the solar system that don't have moons.

- Jupiter, Saturn, Uranus, and Neptune have rings.

- One of Saturn's moons, Mimas, looks like the Death Star from *Star Wars*.

- Uranus is lying on its side.

- Neptune has a dark spot that may be similar to Jupiter's Great Red Spot.

Jupiter

Mars

Earth

Venus

Mercury

The planets that make up our solar system have different sizes and amounts of gravity. On some planets, you'd weigh less than on Earth. On others, you'd weigh more. Journey through the solar system to find out how much a 60-pound kid would weigh on each.* The drawing shows the eight planets and Pluto.

Mercury	Mars	Uranus
23 pounds	23 pounds	53 pounds
Venus	Jupiter	Neptune
54 pounds	142 pounds	68 pounds
Earth	Saturn	Pluto
60 pounds	64 pounds	4 pounds

* Source: exploratorium.edu/ronh/weight

Saturn

Pluto

Neptune

Uranus

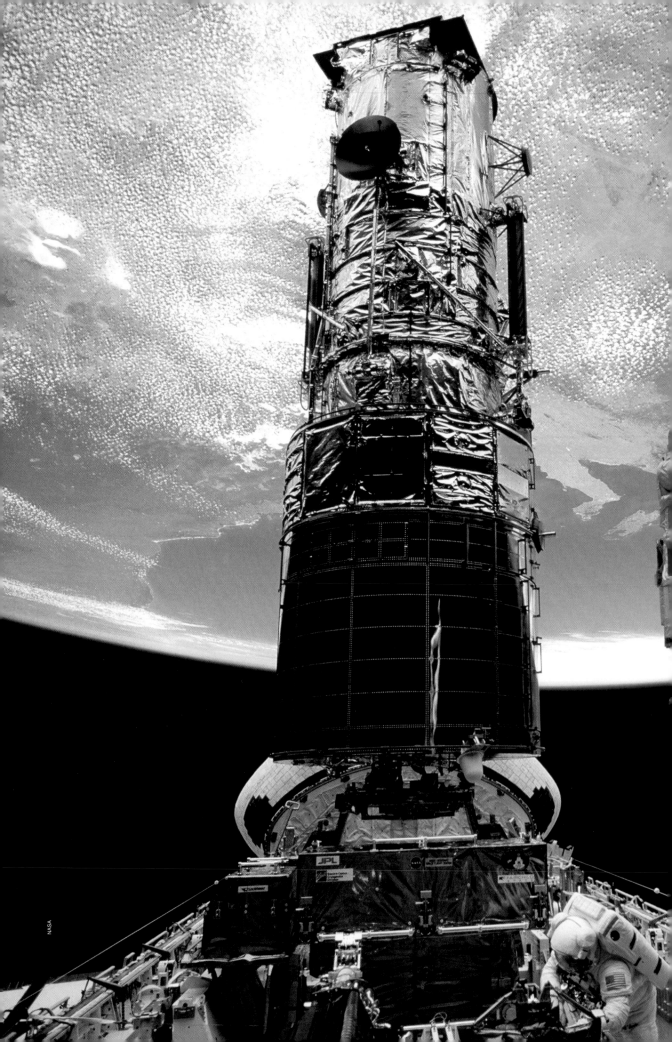

Seeing Into Space

By Ray Villard
Space Telescope Science Institute

Today we know more about Jupiter and the other planets in our solar system than ever before. Yet each day, we get new insights into our solar system—and the universe beyond. What is changing our views of space? The Hubble Space Telescope!

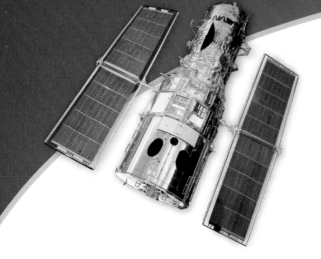

Above It All ▶▶▶▶▶▶▶▶▶

In many ways, Hubble is like any other **telescope.** It simply gathers light. What makes Hubble special is not what it is, but where it is.

Hubble is 350 miles above our planet. It is far from the glare of city lights. Even more important, it's above Earth's atmosphere.

Telescopes on the ground have to look through air. That's not easy. It is sort of like looking through ripples in a pond.

Hubble is above all that. It has a clear view of space. And what a view it is! Hubble is so powerful it could spot a firefly on the moon.

Let's take a look at some of the sights Hubble has glimpsed. We'll start in our solar system. Next we'll move farther into our **galaxy**—the Milky Way. From there, we'll travel to the most distant galaxies in the universe.

Puzzling Planets ▶▶▶▶▶▶▶

You might think that we have found everything in our solar system. It's true that we've seen a lot. But we're still learning more. For example, Pluto is best known as the last planet in our solar system. Yet **astronomers** now say it is not a planet at all.

You see, Pluto is much smaller than the planets in our solar system. It is even smaller than some moons. Pluto is also very icy. No planet is covered in ice like Pluto. So scientists don't think we should call Pluto a planet.

Hubble and other telescopes are finding other icy worlds at the edge of our solar system. One is named Quar. Another is Sedna.

Sedna is three times farther from the sun than Pluto. It is the coldest and most distant known object in our solar system. Sedna takes 10,500 years to circle our sun just once.

So if Pluto is not a planet, what is it? Scientists call Pluto and similar objects **dwarf planets.** These are large objects that are smaller than planets. There may be many dwarf planets out there. The number of planets may be shrinking, but the number of known dwarf planets is growing.

What Makes a Planet?

Is Pluto a planet? Scientists say no. Pluto is smaller than other planets. It is also very icy. Pluto is actually a dwarf planet.

Earth
8,000 miles
in diameter

Moon
2,100 miles
in diameter

Pluto
1,400 miles
in diameter

Sedna
800–1,100 miles
in diameter

Quar
800 miles
in diameter

Exploding Star.
This cloud of gas lies near the edge of the Milky Way galaxy.

Star Gazing ▶ ▶ ▶ ▶ ▶ ▶ ▶ ▶ ▶ ▶ ▶ ▶

Hubble doesn't just focus on our solar system. It also peers into our galaxy and beyond. Many Hubble photos show the stars that make up the Milky Way galaxy. A galaxy is a city of stars.

Nestled among the stars are huge clouds of gas called **nebulae.** Some of these clouds are round. They look like fuzzy planets. But they are really the remains of old stars.

Hubble snapped a photo (above) of one of these gas clouds. The cloud is 20,000 light-years away. A light-year is the distance light travels in one year. Each light-year is about six trillion miles!

A red star marks the cloud's heart. Every once in a while, the star sheds its outer layers of gas. This last happened in 2002.

That year, the normally faint star suddenly brightened. It became one of the brightest stars in the Milky Way. Then it slowly returned to its normal brightness.

Whether it has snapped photos of planets, stars, or galaxies, Hubble has changed the way we look at the universe. Soon, another space telescope will join Hubble above Earth. We can only imagine what new wonders await discovery.

Wordwise

astronomer: space scientist

dwarf planets: large object smaller than a planet

galaxy: system of stars

nebula: cloud of gas in space

telescope: device used to study distant objects

Jupiter

Check out these questions to discover
what you've learned about Jupiter.

1 What planets make up our
solar system?

2 What makes Jupiter different
from these other planets?

3 How long does it take for Jupiter
to revolve around the sun?

4 What are the Galilean moons?
How are they different from
Jupiter's other moons?

5 How has the Hubble Space
Telescope changed the
way we understand
the universe?

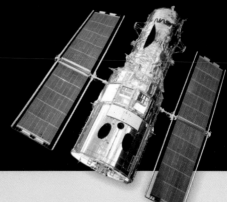